Sarah Whitmer Foster suffered from Early-onset
Alzheimer's Disease from 2004
to her death in May 2015. This work is dedicated to
Sarah and her remarkable compassion for others. May
the Almighty smile upon her.

Permission to use the "tree of life' on the cover has
been granted by Sandy Grant, Phuthadikobo Museum,
P.O. Box 367, Mochudi, Botswana.

AN INTRODUCTION TO CHURCH COUNSELING:

FROM AFRICA, FOR AFRICA

by

Sarah Whitmer Foster, J. T. Foster, Jr., and
Kekelwa Nyaywa-Dall

About the Authors:

This workbook has long-term merit. Written in Gaborone, Botswana, from 1988 to 1989, it was created in an urban center during a time of immense turmoil. Nelson Mandela was still in prison, and violence from the South African Army occurred in the same neighborhood where Sarah and John Foster lived. The Fosters brought an unusual background to Southern Africa. Sarah held a MSW in Social Work and a Ph.D. in International Education/ Development while John combined a graduate background in Cultural Anthropology and Instructional Design. In 1982, five years before coming to Botswana, the Fosters had studied women's groups in Western Province, Kenya. In addition to living in Botswana's capital, experiences with churches in Zimbabwe, South Africa, and Gaborone dramatically enriched their knowledge.

When the Fosters went to live in Botswana, they were on leave from a historically black American university where they had taught thousands of undergraduates. John joined the faculty of Florida A&M in 1971, and Sarah followed him in 1978. Their experiences on this fine campus created a sensitivity and respect for a very diverse population.

After the Fosters returned home to Tallahassee, Florida, an early version of the counseling course presented in the following pages was shared with a variety of African professionals, including a Zambian writer and novelist, Kekelwa Nyaywa-Dall. Sensing the potential of the course, Nyaywa-Dall joined the Fosters' project. Once the three had implemented improvements, the Fosters returned to Africa in 1993 to collect reactions from students and faculty who had used the workbook in Zimbabwe and Botswana. A mixture of forty-eight persons responded to a questionnaire about the counseling course, with 90% believing that the workbook would improve counseling skills—findings the authors published in the *Evangelical Missions Quarterly* in July 1995.

PREFACE

Needs Assessment:

There are situations in Africa which cause both immense suffering and a need for church counseling. In some African locations, unemployment, poverty, social change, violence, alcoholism, and AIDS can accompany the plight of refugees and displaced families. Unemployment rates frequently double those found in the United States during the worst of the 1930s Great Depression. "Despite some positive strides that have been made during the last two decades in HIV/AIDS testing, prevention, and treatment, Sub-Sahara Africa is a center of the HIV/AIDS pandemic. In 2013 an estimated 24.7 million people in this region were living with HIV, accounting for 71% of the global total." (Source: UNAIDS Data 2017)

The capacity of churches to respond to these problems is often limited. The average pastor or church leader in Africa has not attended a seminary. Among those who have gone to such schools, many have attended programs which place little emphasis upon practical theology and counseling. The same trend continues even in extension education. One of the most commonly used set of texts includes "no books on counseling."[1]

Background:

In 1987 and 1988, African clergy in Botswana identified a need for training in basic counseling skills. Their request to address this need led to the design of this workbook. A draft completed in 1990 has been used at Kgolagano College, Botswana's School of Theological Education by Extension. In 1993 this workbook was also adopted as a text by the Baptist Seminary in Gweru, Zimbabwe. In the same year, the authors returned to those schools and collected evaluations from students and faculty. Evaluations were also obtained from African clergy and also several career missionaries. Of the 48 respondents, 43 (89.6 percent) recommended that this workbook be used in extension education, 45 persons (93.7 percent) believed it could be used to improve the skills of clergy, and 44 (91.7 percent) encouraged its use in seminaries. Letters of commendation recommending the workbook have been received from Baptists, Mennonites, Lutherans, Presbyterians, Methodists, Anglicans and Catholics. Additionally, Desmond M. Tutu, Archbishop Emeritus, sent in 1999 his own compliments to the authors.[2]

Methodology and Effectiveness:

This workbook uses case studies to portray some of the struggles of life—adjusting to living in a city, feelings at the death of a parent, and others. Problems are described as they often come to counselors, without quick answers. The simple telling of one's story to a thoughtful listener can result in spiritual and psychological insight and healing. A concern for listening is, of course, African, and it is important in both customary law and traditional healing. After studying the relationships between traditional healers and their clients, Uba came to believe that listening was "the core" of traditional helping.[3] The importance of listening also appears in still other works by Cole by Berinyuu, and also by the Catholic bishops of Uganda in their "Pastoral Letter on AIDS." "The caregiver can listen with empathy to the spoken words and the non-spoken signs of the client."[4]

While a combination of listening with descriptions of current problems offers ways to adapt the workbook's content to the cultural setting, the lessons are also structured to reflect cultural patterns. Information is exchanged orally. It has been the custom in Africa "to share the news" after friends greet each other. In using brief case studies or small stories, the lessons reflect established patterns of sharing and listening in everyday life. As a result, this workbook is contextualized in two dimensions, including content and process.

While this workbook provides an extraordinary response to the requests of African clergy, important issues remain. The authors were not asked to invent new theory, so they used the ideas of Carl Rogers. More useful theory can and should be developed in Africa. Still other improvements can be made, and the authors hope that you will make them.

1. Stewart G. Snook, *Developing Leaders Through Theological Education by Extension (Wheaton: 1992), 104.*
2. A published article about this workbook appeared in the *Evangelical Missions Quarterly* (July 1995), 302-8. The workbook's original title was *An Introduction to Pastoral Counseling: From Africa, For Africa.* Archbishop Tutu sent a letter to Sarah and John Foster dated February 23, 1999.
3. Anselm Uba, "Counseling in the Present African Context," *African Christian Studies 7* (Sept. 1991), 54-73.
4. Victor Cole, "Concepts of Pastoral Leadership in Africa: a Case Study," *Africa Journal of Evangelical Theology* 2 (1990), 3-11; A. A. Berinyuu, The Encounter of Western Civilization and Islam on Ghanaian Culture: Implications for the Ministry of Pastoral Care and Counseling." *Africa Theological Journal* 17 (1988), 143-49. Catholic Bishops of Uganda, "Message on the AIDS Epidemic." *African Ecclesial Review* 1 (Oct. 1988), 289-30.

Introduction:

The following lessons are intended to provide an introduction to church counseling for persons who live in Africa and also for those who are involved with Africans abroad. This workbook is intended as a beginning look at an important form of ministry.

For the purposes of this workbook the following definition is suggested: "church counseling" is a process which occurs between a pastor [or elder or deacon or teacher] and a person or family, during which concerns or problems are identified and explored. The purpose of this sharing is to encourage the growth and well-being of parishioners. Counseling requires a person who can listen, be non-judgmental, and keeps the content of the interaction private. A church member with training in counseling listens as individuals and families share their needs. By sharing needs with a thoughtful listener, creative answers can emerge.

Comments About Theory:

Careful listening occurs in many traditional African cultures. When problems are brought to chiefs and elders, good listening is important. In customary law leaders are expected to hear descriptions of events and note variations in testimony. At the same time, listening is also a foundation of counseling, and attentive listening is therefore an important theme throughout this workbook.

Other traditional practices, more directive and prescriptive, can also be useful. Tradition can provide valuable answers. Yet in many places, workable solutions may require going beyond tradition, seeking help from a variety of sources. The overall goal of this workbook is to support the efforts of Africans — indeed, of all people—to live meaningfully, as whole people, as children of God.

Comments to Non-African Readers:

The concerns of Africans are not always the same as those of North Americans, Europeans, or people from other non-African cultures. Consequently, African topics, such as ancestors and their effects upon the living, appear in the coming pages. So, too, does the issue of polygamy. Readers who find these topics "strange" or "peculiar" are encouraged to remember that the behaviours of North Americans and Europeans may look "strange" or "peculiar" to other people. Both Americans and Europeans often stress the importance of the individual at the expense of families and the community. Yet, many Americans seem perplexed at the troubles overwhelming their own families. It is important to understand behaviour within a cultural setting without condemning that behaviour. Try to recognize biased or ethnocentric reactions and guard against them.

Pronunciation Note:

Residents of Botswana pronounce a written "G" as "H." The written name Gaborone, the capital of Botswana, is pronounced as "Haboronē," not "Gaboron."

LESSON 1

AFRICA AND CHANGE

Life in Africa is changing. "The urban population growth rate averages almost 5 percent per year over the last two decades. On average the population of the Africa Region is now one-third urbanized (a proportion higher than South Asia's 28 percent)."

City life confronts people with new problems. Many traditional ideas and beliefs don't always provide answers for new situations. Worry, sadness, and stress are common feelings. Behind these emotions are basic problems — joblessness, inadequate housing, and a lack of money. The pressures of change and city life increase alcoholism, crime, marital problems, and violence.

A study by lecturers at the University of Zimbabwe revealed that "one in every four patients visiting a clinic complaining of physical pain actually suffers from 'hidden' emotional problems."[1] The most common problems suffered by these people were anxiety and depression, often brought on by family or financial problems. Men complained of unemployment; divorce; payment of lobola, or bride prices; and the death of close relatives. Women's problems centered around difficult marriage or family relationships. They worried about lack of money, infertility, and second or third wives being introduced into the household.[2]

Questions:

1. What were the causes of hidden emotional problems among many people?

2. The list of causes for hidden emotional problems is not complete. Of the problems concerning men, what are some that were not named?

3. Of the problems concerning women, what are some that were not named?

Notes 1-2 are from "Hidden Mental Illness is Harming Zimbabwe's Health Care," *The Star* (Johannesburg), Sept. 21, 1988.

LESSON 2

WHEN COUNSELING IS NEEDED

The study in Zimbabwe also described how clinics responded to anxiety and depression. Clinic staffs often failed to understand what really made people feel "weak, dizzy or generally painful" or tired.[3] As a result, people with emotional problems were treated with pain killers and cough mixtures. Such treatment does not lead to positive change. Consequently, many persons with emotional problems kept coming back to the clinics looking for help.

Most of the people in this study needed someone to talk to. "Many benefited from simply talking about their problems."[4] Some people have such a great need for listening that they share their problems in newspapers. One letter sent to a newspaper for advice begins: "I'm a man of 27 and I am in love with my wife's sister."

In a typical congregation, there are those who need a good listener. Some have broken marriages. Others have lost children to alcohol or to crime. The church cannot turn away from their needs. For Christianity to be alive in us means that we are called to reach out to those in need, those who suffer.

The purpose of this course is to introduce learners to counseling — one of the basic ways of healing the sick. As Africa continues to change, the need for counseling is likely to increase.

Questions:

1. Name the ways that some clinics responded to anxiety and depression.

2. What actually made people with emotional problems feel better?

3. What is the relationship between counseling and suffering?

4. What concerns might members of your congregation share with a good listener?

Notes 3-4 are from "Hidden Mental Illness is Harming Zimbabwe's Health Care."

LESSON 3

WHAT ARE CASE STUDIES?

Case studies or case histories are very useful in the study of counseling. A case study describes parts of a person's life, including a group of events that are related to each other. Case studies can be used to describe how a person's problems came about, when various things happened and how people reacted to important events. Counseling is about helping people overcome their problems, and case studies are both a way to record problems and important information related to them.

Case studies, when carefully written, can be used for analysis and understanding. They are not unlike stories and folk tales that have been told in parts of Africa. A good case study like a good story can reveal some basic truth. This course uses many case studies for discussion. The next lesson about a man, Thabo, is an example of a case study. We hope you will find this to be an interesting way to learn.

Questions:

1. What are some uses for case studies in counseling?

LESSON 4

CASE STUDY 1: THABO, A PERSON SEEKING HELP

Thabo came to the city looking for work. With the drought at his village, he felt he never was going to have cattle or money. How could he ever marry Ketsile? Thabo wanted to do things the right way and to marry her properly.

Life in the city was confusing. People do not greet each other. Jobs are not easy to find. People keep telling Thabo there is no work. The rents are so high Thabo stays with his cousin, Tiro. Tiro is unhappy with his job and his house in a squatter camp. Besides, Tiro drinks too much beer and fights with his girlfriend. One night Tiro locked her out of his house. She screamed at him and kept hitting the door with her fist. Tiro just turned on the radio and drank more beer.

After three weeks of living with Tiro, Thabo is discouraged and feels awful. Walking along the street behind the post office, Thabo saw a man who was well dressed. It was Deacon Taumotho. Thabo started talking with him and began to explain his unhappiness. Deacon Taumotho listened for a minute and said, "Life is hard for many people. You should go home and pray. Ask God to help you."

This made Thabo feel good for an hour or so. That night Tiro was madder than ever. His girlfriend had an old lover in Tiro's house, and Tiro had found them together. The noise and yelling was worse than ever. Tiro hit her on the head with a bottle. Thabo felt he had to leave the house. So he spent the night sleeping on the ground under a piece of plastic.

This morning Thabo saw a man hide a pair of new shoes under his jacket and walk out of a store. "Is that what a person must do to live in a city?" Thabo thought.

Questions:

1. A case study is part of a person's life. Write or describe an event in your life that could be shared with others. What happened? When? How did you feel about it?

LESSON 5

BEING A GOOD LISTENER: THE BEGINNING OF COUNSELING

In the first case study, Thabo is like many people. He has problems which affect his life. How he solves them can have a major impact on his future. Thabo's life could be very different if he is patient, and he finds work. He might even be able to earn enough money to marry the woman he loves. On the other hand, Thabo could gradually turn to crime or to alcohol as Tiro has. Thabo's choices could lead to success and honor or eventually to the police station and prison.

At times, people with problems try to talk about their difficulties with other people. Thabo did this when he saw church Deacon Taumotho. Counseling can begin when one person shares their worries, concerns and fears with someone who is a thoughtful listener. Deacon Taumotho was given a chance to be a counselor but he did not give Thabo enough time to meaningfully share his problems. He was not a good listener. Later that night, sleeping under the plastic, Thabo felt awful.

Counseling involves thoughtful listening—that is, listening to what someone is saying and giving them a chance to find their own answers. The act of listening allows the expression of problems and feelings—first steps in understanding. In that way, people overcome obstacles to their personal growth. It is a time in which a person learns more about themselves and their life. Counseling should increase a person's understanding of problems and lead to decisions which reduce difficulties.

Questions:

1. What choice or choices is Thabo making? Why are they important?

2.   What can be achieved in counseling?

3. What Deacon Taumotho said to Thabo is not counseling. Name two reasons why it was not counseling.

LESSON 6

WHY COUNSELING IS NEEDED IN AFRICA

Many newspapers, magazines and books written about Africa describe major problems. The size of these problems and their effects upon people all suggest the need for counseling:

1. "On World Humanitarian Day 2017, Africa's population displacement crisis has reached record levels, with over 20 million Africans now officially registered as refugees, internally displaced, or seeking asylum." Displaced persons are still in their country of residence. Yet they cannot stay in their homes because of violence or natural disasters.[1]

2. Poverty is very common and affects much of the population of Africa. "In 2010, 414 million people were living in extreme poverty across sub-Saharan Africa."[2]

3. Unemployment is very high. Even in a country with a growing economy such as Botswana's, unemployment exceeds 17%. In Zimbabwe unemployment might reach several times that amount.[3]

4. "AIDS is disproportionately effecting Africans more than other people in the rest of the world, with HIV accounting for more than 70% of the global infection rate."[4]

5. Violence within families is common. Statistics released in Zimbabwe suggest that eight out of ten women experience violence in their homes. Much of this is blamed on "male drunkenness."[5] Drinking also accounts for half of all fatal vehicle accidents among countries located in the region.

Many major problems can cause feelings of sadness or gloom. They can lead to worry and fear, or even anger. When people live for extended periods with such emotions, they may need help through counseling.

Questions:

1. Look at the problems in this lesson. How common are these in your city, town or village?

2. What are some important problems which seem to bother people you know?

3. How do people feel about these problems? What emotions do they show?

1. reliefweb.int/report/world/africa-s-population-displacement-
       reaches-record-levels-2017
2. borgenproject.org/10-quick-facts-about-poverty-in-africa/
3. tradingeconomics.com/botswana/unemployment-rate
4. www.ncbi.nlm.nih.gov/pmc/articles/PMC4893541/
5. Bulawayo (Zimbabwe) *Chronicle*, March 11, 1988.

LESSON 7

CASE STUDY 2: TIRO'S COUNSELING BEGINS

Tiro's drinking continued to get worse, and it began to worry him. At times he no longer remembered what he did or said. While he did not like his job at least he had one. Recently the manager saw Tiro drinking at work. "Tiro, you are a good worker. If you weren't I would sack you this very minute. You must not drink around the equipment. Stop doing it."

Troubled and anxious, Tiro went to see Rre (Mr.) Matumo at his old school. Rre Matumo was one of the best teachers Tiro ever had. Rre Matumo was rather old and very wise, and Tiro liked his teacher's knowledge of the world. "Rre Matumo knows almost everything."

After greeting his teacher, Tiro began talking to Rre Matumo. Rre Matumo was happy to see his old student. "Tiro, how are you doing? You look worried." Over the next ten or fifteen minutes Tiro began to explain how he started drinking. He began going to a nearby *shebeen,* or tavern, because he was lonely. Now he went because he liked the taste of alcohol. It was not easy for Tiro to say these things. Yet as he did, he began to feel a little better.

After a long time Rre Matumo said, "You have a very real enemy. Alcohol steals your money, and it could steal your life. My own brother was killed when his *kombi* (van) turned over. He had been drinking late one Saturday night. You need to think about what to do."

Then Tiro remembered seeing a notice about Alcoholics Anonymous* and its meetings at one of the churches. Rre Matumo," said Tiro, "what do you think about it?"

Rre Matumo said it might help. "You could try it. If you do, come back and tell me what it's like."

When Tiro left his old teacher he was feeling better. "Perhaps I can do something about by problem."

Questions:

1. Why was the manager concerned about Tiro's drinking problem?

2. What did Rre Matumo tell Tiro about his own brother?

3. How could Alcoholics Anonymous be helpful to Tiro?

*Alcoholics Anonymous is a support group for people with a drinking problem. By sharing their common concerns, group participants can help each other.

LESSON 8

COUNSELING BEGINS: A BRIEF DISCUSSION

Because Rre (Mr.) Matumo is a good listener, Tiro could talk to him and express how he felt. Counseling gives a person like Tiro the chance to explore his feelings. As Tiro began to think of ways to deal with his drinking problem, he became more hopeful.

Tiro respected Rre Matumo and his knowledge of the world. Rre Matumo was concerned and listened thoughtfully, giving his friend Tiro time to find his own answers. Whenever and wherever counseling occurs, the quality of the relationship between people is very important.

Questions:

1. Counseling requires more than just a few minutes of discussion. Why?

2. Tiro went to see Rre Matumo because his old teacher was a special person. Why might someone want to share problems with Rre Matumo?

3. Have you shared a problem with someone you know? Describe this person.

LESSON 9

EFFECTIVE COUNSELORS

Respect, trust, empathy and the ability to listen are traits that many effective counselors have. These qualities are evident when counselors listen and talk with others. Rre Matumo, in his conversation with Tiro, is no exception.

Respect implies high regard. Tiro valued Rre Matumo for his age, wisdom, and knowledge of the world. He did not take his problem to just anyone.

Trust combines hope and confidence. Because a person has knowledge does not mean they will know how to use it, or use it in the best way. Tiro hoped that Rre Matumo would listen to his problem and react with his ideas. Tiro's trust in Rre Mature was not misplaced. The old teacher was happy to see Tiro, and he was honest in what he said.

Empathy is the ability to see and to understand what another person is feeling. Rre Matumo recognized the seriousness of alcoholism. He wished his own brother had stopped drinking — he might still be alive. Rre Matumo's words show empathy, "You have a very real enemy. Alcohol steals your money, and it could steal your life."

Lastly, Rre Matumo has the ability to listen. Listening is the most important of all counseling skills. In his meeting with Tiro, the teacher did very little talking. Rre Matumo was interested in his old student, and he really wanted to hear what Tiro had to say. A person who talks all of the time never hears the worries and problems of others. He is like a calabash, already full of water. Such a person is full of his own thoughts and feelings. He can hold nothing more.

Questions:

1. List four qualities that are common among effective counselors.

2. In the first case study, Lesson 4, Rev. Taumotho does not show much empathy for Thabo. What could Rev. Taumotho have said which would have shown more empathy? Write your suggestion.

3. In what ways does Rre Matumo show his empathy for Tiro? Mark places in the case study in which Rre Matumo shows his understanding of Tiro's problem.

LESSON 10

CASE STUDY 3: COUNSELING AND CONFIDENTIALITY

At tea Rre Matumo started talking with another teacher, Mma (Mrs.) Brown. Rre Matumo began to describe his morning: "The students seem very excited about the coming holiday."

After a while, Mma Brown mentioned Tiro. "Didn't I see you talking with him? Tiro could have been a better student if he had worked harder. Knowing him, he has probably gotten into trouble."

Rre Matumo thought about telling Mma Brown about Tiro's drinking. Then he decided not to tell her. He thought, "Mma Brown talks about all the students and their problems. Yet she does not seem to help them. Tiro's problem is important. It is not just something to make people laugh. Besides, if lots of people knew about Tiro this might upset him. Alcoholism is enough trouble."

Rre Matumo only mentioned Tiro's job in the old industrial park, and then he returned to talking about the holiday.

Questions:

1.   This case study does not explain why Mma Brown knows Tiro. Why does she probably know him?

2.   Apply the qualities of an effective counselor to Mma Brown. Which are her weak ones?

LESSON 11

A DISCUSSION OF CONFIDENTIALITY

Most counselors do not share information they learn about another person, like Tiro, with just anyone. Knowledge about the problems, fears, worries of others can be used for many purposes — both good and bad. Tiro shared his concerns with Rre Matumo because he wanted help and advice. Had he wanted to amuse Mma Brown, Tiro would have talked with her. By not telling Mma Brown, Rre Matumo protected both Tiro and the information Tiro had shared. The trust Tiro had for Rre Matumo was very well placed. Information learned in counseling is not public information to be retold.

Information has the power to destroy. Note John 18, verse 2. To avoid misuse of information, a counselor should not talk about things learned while counseling. Any exceptions to this rule could be approved by the person who is the source of the information. If Tiro wants his problem shared, he is the person to share it or give permission for others to share it.

Questions:

1. Information learned in counseling is confidential. Look up this word in a dictionary. What does "confidential" mean? Write a definition based on your experience.

2. Have you ever seen information misused because some-one talked too much? What happened?

LESSON 12

AGAPE, A FOUNDATION OF CHURCH COUNSELING

At the centre of church counseling is *agape* (ah-gah-pay), the Greek word for Christian love. Christ commands us to love our neighbor. It is to be applied to sinners, like the woman at the well and even to hated tax collectors. Christ's love extended to all, even those beyond his family and friends. The Samaritans (Luke 12:6-7) and other enemies of the Jews were worthy, in the eyes of Jesus, of love. The commandment to love others includes even our enemies. (Luke 6:27)

Counseling is a way to express agape, to say to those who are troubled that they are loved. Love permits others to share their pain and suffering. Problems are to be heard with compassion. Through loving listening, people like Tiro begin to find answers. The foundation for church counseling is agape.

Questions

1. In Case Study 3, Mma Brown does not express agape. If she had expressed agape towards Tiro, what might she have said?

2. In what ways do Rre Matumo's thoughts or actions express agape?

3. This lesson does not name all the parts of scripture which show agape. What are some others which show agape?

LESSON 13

CHURCH LEADERS AS SHEPHERDS

You may have wondered why ministers and church leaders are at times called <u>Pastors</u>. The word pastor is from the Old Testament and New Testament understanding of the word "shepherd." A shepherd is one who has been given the responsibility of looking after the sheep. That is, one who feeds them, one who protects the weak, one who heals the sick and who searches for the lost ones (Ezekiel 34:1-4). In the Old Testament the Psalmist refers to God as my "Shepherd" (Ps. 23:1). In the gospel according to Matthew it is recorded how Jesus saw the crowds and "his heart was filled with pity for them, for they were like sheep without a shepherd" (Matt. 9:36). In John, Jesus is described as the "Good Shepherd" (John 10:11). And lastly, Jesus, after the resurrection, called Peter to "Feed my lambs...Tend my sheep...Feed my sheep" (John 21:115-17).

Jesus compared the people to sheep and himself to a shepherd. It is for this reason that ministers and church leaders who look after the people and their needs are called "pastors," and by doing this they shared in the pastoral concerns of the flock—the people of God.

While pastors and church leaders are called to look after people and their needs, this is not always easy. One finds in villages, cities and towns many different people.

* How can I as the shepherd look after the man who curses the boy begging in the street for a piece of bread?

* How can I look after the woman who starts a rumor of "bad magic" which eventually leads to the burning of a neighbor's house?

* How can I look after the school girl who sleeps with almost any man for money for school fees and uniforms?

What we are called to do as Christians is not always easy. Yet Jesus has shared with us a simple but important message: Christian love must extend to the Christian fellowship, to the neighbor, to the enemy and to all the world. Turning this message into action means that we are capable, with God's help, of finding ways to look after people and their needs, no matter who they are or what they have done to themselves or others.[1]

Questions:

1. What are the duties of shepherds?

2. Can you think of other scripture where shepherds are important? Name them.

3. How can you use Christ's message of love in looking after people and their needs? Write an example.

1. This discussion is an edited version of pages from earlier Kgolagano counseling courses. Permission granted by Kgolagano College, Gaborone, Botswana.

LESSON 14

THE RESPONSIBILITIES OF SHEPHERDS

Jesus, the Chief Shepherd, gave a three-fold command to all who follow him: to preach the gospel, to teach and to heal the sick. It is an accepted fact that the church—through her worship, preaching, Sunday schools, youth work and the sacraments— serves a valuable purpose in the lives of the believers. Yet the church often fails to see its responsibility to personal needs within the fellowship of the church. A sensitive pastor or elder should, looking at a congregation, see many whose lives hide deep wounds and heavy burdens. As you examine a congregation, you may see a man whose wife was admitted to the mental hospital, a person deeply in debt because of a gambling habit, a young wife deeply depressed by the tragic death of her first child, and Tiro's girlfriend with an ugly cut on her forehead. As a church leader it is important to remember the message of love and the command to heal the sick.[1]

Questions:

1. The need for healing is felt in all of a person's life. Grief, fear, and worry —like fever or broken bones — need healing too. Has someone ever reduced your fears or worries or helped you in a time of great sadness? What did they say or do?

2. In what ways have you been a "Good Shepherd?"

3. Have you ever had an opportunity to be a "Good Shepherd" and missed it?

1. Permission granted by Kgologano College, Gaborone, Botswana.

LESSON 15

COUNSELING

Preaching to the converted does not fulfill God's plan, the plan of salvation and redemption for the "whole" person. Many people today believe preaching to crowds as an attempt to fill a number of bottles by flinging a bucketful of water over them. What is needed, they argue, is that each bottle be attended to separately and personally to get good results. In other words, church counseling is concerned about each person as a person.

Church counseling carries on the work of Jesus as individuals face problems in everyday life. People need healing to become "whole" by going beyond their previous conditions. They need sustenance, spiritual food, to defeat the problems that seem impossible to overcome. They need guidance to be able to make choices. And lastly, they need to be reconciled with themselves, others, and God. Broken relationships need to be mended. Such people need someone who can listen, feel and relate to their problems. The church counselor practices what is known as "reflective listening." Reflective listeners hear both the feelings and the words of other people and reflect them back.

Many people are looking for an ear that will listen. They do not find one because so many are talking when they should be listening. He or she who no longer listens to their neighbor will soon no longer be listening to God. Through counseling many people who are depressed and in conflict find release from their fears and spiritual uncertainties. Church counseling is an expression of faith in service, and helps people to increase their ability to love God and their neighbor.[1]

Questions:

1. What is church counseling? Look again at the introduction to this workbook. Apply it to your congregation.

2. Name three goals of church counseling.

3. Is counseling taking place in your own congregation? If so, by whom and how? If not, why not?

1. Permission granted by Kgolagano College, Gaborone, Botswana.

LESSON 16

CASE STUDY 4: SEEKING COUNSELING

In the early 1970s, Rre Matumo's brother, Benson, had a girlfriend. Benson thought he loved her very much, and he made lots of promises. "I will marry you as soon as I finish my education."

Benson was surprised at his high marks on his "A" levels. Within months he found himself at a university hundreds of kilometers from home. His studies were very demanding, and the work took all of his time. He gave little thought to his girlfriend.

A month later, she wrote Benson saying that she was pregnant. When he read her letter he became very upset. He tore up the letter and threw away the pieces. "I will find another woman when I go back home."

At university, Benson's grades were not good, and his teachers criticized his work. Benson began to think that his ancestors were unhappy, and he began to feel guilty about the trouble he had caused his girlfriend. Her parents had been shamed, and they were not bad people.

Benson once tried to tell his feelings to a social worker he knew. The social worker didn't realize the importance of ancestors, and could not understand Benson's growing feelings of fear.

Questions:

1. Why was Benson afraid?

2. If Benson had shared his worries with you, what could you say to him?

LESSON 17

DIFFERENCES BETWEEN TYPES OF COUNSELING

There are many different kinds of counselors and counseling. Church counseling, in its emphasis on wholeness, includes spiritual concerns. Had Benson gone to a pastor, the issue of forgiveness and being made new would have been more likely to occur. Some types of counselors and counseling tend to be less concerned with spiritual life and our relationship to God.

Questions:

1. What does "wholeness" mean? Look it up in a dictionary and write a definition. What does "being whole" mean to you?

2. Name two differences between church counseling and other forms of counseling.

LESSON 18

CHRIST'S CONCERN FOR THE PERSON

While the Gospels are a record of Christ's public ministry, they also tell of his concern for the person. People with problems did not go ignored even when there were crowds. The little Zacchaeus, a tax collector, climbed a tree. Yet Christ's eye did not see just the multitude. "He looked up and said to him, 'Zacchaeus, make haste and come down, for I must stay at your house today.'" (Luke 19:5--6)

At other times, individuals brought their concerns and questions directly to Christ — who, in turn, responded to them. Foremost among these, of course, was Nicodemus, who "came by night." And when he didn't understand Christ's answers, Nicodemus asked still other questions. (John 3:1-15)

At times, the person with spiritual needs was healed in the presence of people who did not understand. The sinful woman anointed Christ's feet with ointment and tears. Christ said to the Pharisees, "Her sins, which are many, are forgiven." "And he said to her, 'Your sins are forgiven.'" (Luke 7:36-50)

Jesus understood the needs of the multitudes without losing the needs of each person. In Christ's ministry children, the tax collector and the woman of Samaria were all important. In the example of the woman at the well, the disciples arrived only at the end of the conversation. (See John 4:27) Yet the water of life had already been shared.

Questions:

1. Reread your definition of counseling (Lesson 15).

2. Christ addressed personal needs in still other situations. Name another situation.

3. How was Jesus able to address both the needs of the individual and the multitude?

LESSON 19

CASE STUDY 5: AN EXAMPLE OF CHURCH COUNSELING

Benson's distress continued to grow, and he eventually talked about his problems to one of the few students he knew at the university. The student, Molefe, realized that Benson needed some help. Molefe encouraged Benson to see Rev. Moore.

Benson was not pleased with the idea of talking to a *moruti* (pastor). Yet neither was Benson content with doing nothing. While he wanted help he didn't want to hear more about Christianity.

Despite his uncertainty, Benson decided to tell Rev. Moore about his fear of his ancestors and his girlfriend's pregnancy. "If he does not want to hear about these things, then he does not want to hear about me," he thought.

As Benson began talking, Rev. Moore didn't interrupt him. The pastor didn't fully understand Benson's concern about his dead relatives. He was trying to learn, and he began to wonder, "Why are your ancestors so unhappy if you are the first in your family to go to university? Why aren't they proud of you?"

Despite his discomfort, Rev. Moore continued to listen to Benson without saying he didn't understand. Moore thought to himself, "How can I help a lost sheep if I drive him away at the beginning?"

Benson went on to describe his bad luck in the city. "I have only trouble here. And nothing is going well at home. My girlfriend is pregnant. I thought I loved her but now I don't." Eventually, Benson asked Rev. Moore what he should do about his girlfriend. The pastor looked at him and said, "What do you think, Benson? What might make the situation better?"

Questions:

1.   Why didn't Benson like the student Molefe's advice?

2.   What might Benson have done if Rev. Moore criticized him? What seems likely?

3.   Apply the qualities of effective counselors to Rev. Moore. What are his strengths? What are his weaknesses? (You may need to take another look at Lesson 9.)

LESSON 20

BASIC GOALS

Counseling implies a relationship between people in which the person with problems feels free to talk about these problems. This means that the counselor listens without rejecting or condemning. Discussing problems can give rise to talking about solutions. Talking about problems and implementing solutions can lead to understanding and growth — basic goals of counseling. In Christ's own ministry, he showed love, compassion and understanding for the hungry, lame, and grieving.

Questions:

1.   Counseling is not based upon condemning or criticizing. What scripture would support such practices?

2.   How might Benson have answered Rev. Moore's last question?

LESSON 21

SOME RESULTS

After talking with Rev. Moore, Benson continued to think about ways to make the situation with girlfriend better. Everyone back home knew that her baby was his. Benson was looking for reconciliation.

Over the passage of months, friendship grew between Benson and Rev. Moore. At the same time, Benson's unwillingness to hear about Christianity gradually went away.

Questions:

1.   What is reconciliation? Define it.

2.   Reconciliation is important to Christians. What is an example of reconciliation in the New Testament?

3.   What could Benson have done as an act of reconciliation?

LESSON 22

USEFUL COUNSELING SKILLS

Whether a person is a Rre Matumo or a Rev. Moore, counselors need skills. These skills can be learned. Many experts believe that some of the most important skills are listed below:
1. Observe
2. Listen
3. Question
4. Clarify
5. Summarize

Now let's look at each skill a little more closely:

1. Observe the other person's behaviour, how they act. What expressions and gestures do they use to show how they feel?

2. Listen carefully to everything that they tell you. Sometimes little things are most important.

3. Question thoughtfully to learn more about the other person's situation, problem or concern.

4. Clarify what is not understood. That is, ask the person to explain something you find confusing or unclear.

5. Summarize what has been said by the person who has come to see you, and the what you have said in response. It can be helpful to review what has been said.

Questions:

1. How do you know that someone is listening to what you are saying? Give examples.

2. Write, in your words, a definition of what is meant by summary.

3. Look up "clarify" in the dictionary and write the definition that is the most appropriate one for use in a counseling course.

LESSON 23

EXAMPLES OF COUNSELING SKILLS: OBSERVING AND LISTENING

<u>OBSERVING</u>

People communicate about themselves through their appearance, expressions and actions. An effective observer learns to watch carefully to learn more about the concerns a person is bringing to the counselor.

KETSILE

Ketsile walked in very slowly. Her head was bowed, her dress dirty. She sat down in the chair but did not lift her head very often. She gazed most of the time at the floor. Her voice was so quiet that it was very difficult to hear what she was saying. Sometimes she would repeat a word two or three times, seeming to forget what she was saying. At times, she shifted from one side of the chair to the other.

<u>LISTENING</u>

Listening is both a quality needed in counseling and a basic skill. Not everyone listens effectively to others, but it is a skill that can be learned.

PETER

Yesterday someone broke into Peter's house. Many things were stolen. He had bought a new tape recorder for his children for Christmas. That was gone. Also missing were several tapes — stories that his children loved. All of this has made Peter angry.

Questions:

1. What is Ketsile communicating in her actions rather than in words? What did she do when she came into the room?

2. Can you remember learning a lot about a person by observing that person? Write what you learned.

3. If you had been listening to Peter, what would you have learned from what he said?

4. What would you like to know that Peter did not tell you.

LESSON 24

**EXAMPLES OF COUNSELING SKILLS:
QUESTIONING, CLARIFYING AND SUMMARIZING**

<u>QUESTIONING</u>

To learn more from Peter, you ask questions. We learn about the lives of people and the events that affect them by asking questions.

PETER

I asked Peter about the break in. He told me... A) That it occurred while all of the family was away B) No neighbor heard any noise. C) They discovered things missing soon after coming home.

<u>CLARIFYING</u>

Some times people share with us information that we don't completely understand. Further questioning can prevent misunderstanding and help lead to a solution.

KETSILE

When Ketsile finally talked she mentioned feeling sick in the morning. I asked, "Ketsile, does this happen every morning? Is it before breakfast or afterwards?"

<u>SUMMARIZING</u>

This is a chance to bring together what has been said. If you were listening to Peter, you could summarize by saying that his house was broken into while everyone was away. No neighbor heard the break in and that missing items noted soon after Peter came home.

Questions:

1. What questions could you have asked to get responses A, B and C from Peter?

2. Write three questions that would clarify, in your mind, why Ketsile has come to you for help.

3. Write a summary of what you know about Ketsile.

LESSON 25

CASE STUDY 6: PROBLEMS IN A FAMILY

Neo and Rose are having problems. They have been living together for five years, at least for much of the time. Rose works in the city for several people, cleaning, ironing and cooking. Of course, she has her own children to take care as well. Betty and Morwadi are in primary school. Betty is seven years old and Morwadi is eight. Neo used to work in the city. But he was offered a job which requires living and traveling in the rural areas. Since his salary would increase by 50 percent, Neo took the new job. Now he travels a lot going from one distant place to another. This has not been easy for him or Rose. Sometimes he comes to the city on the weekend to find Rose not at home. Neo gets angry. When she returns, they argue. Sometimes he beats her. Rose is upset and doesn't know what to do. Neo's parents are dead, and Rose's father has never liked Neo. Rose thought, "Who can I go to other than my pastor or an elder? I am so very sad."

Questions:

1.   Name the problems Neo and Rose are facing.

2.   Why didn't Rose go to her father? Why didn't she talk with Neo's parents?

3.   Why did Neo take the new job?

4.   Write four questions that you would ask Rose — four questions that would give you additional information about her situation.

LESSON 26

DIALOGUE 1: A CONVERSATION ABOUT FAMILY PROBLEMS

While you read about Rose and Neo, what would it be like to actually listen to Rose as she explained the situation to a church elder, Mma Tau? Let's practice observing, listening, questioning, clarifying and summarizing. Here is a dialogue, one that could have taken place:

Mma Tau: Come in. How are you, mma?

Rose: I am not very good. I am worried about my husband.

Mma Tau: Why are you worried?

Rose: Neo has a job away from the city. Sometimes when he comes on the weekends, I am not there. He is very jealous. Neo thinks that I am with another man. I cannot make him believe that I am running errands and not seeing other men. Since he has been hitting me, the children have become afraid of him. They hide when they hear Neo shouting. I am so worried.

Mma Tau: You have a cut above your right eye. Did Neo do this?

Rose: Yes. It is a shame. I have done nothing bad.

Mma Tau: How often does this happen?

Rose: He has been home the last two weekends, and it has happened each time.

Mmq Tau: Would he talk with me if I came to your place?

Rose: I think he would. He said that you are a "good grand-mother."

Mma Tau: Would it be all right for me to come on Saturday? It will just be a visit. I will not talk about his hitting you, just visit. Is there any chance he will be home?

Rose: Yes, I think Neo will come this Saturday.

Mma Tau: I am glad that you came to see me. By explaining Neo's work and how he reacts when he doesn't find you at home, you have helped me understand your situation better. I will come on Saturday.

Rose: Thank you. Goodbye.

Mma Tau: Thank you, mma. Goodbye.

Questions:

1. There are places in the dialogue where the counselor may have been using the five counseling skills — observing, listening, questioning, clarifying and summarizing.

Mark these places with an "O" for observing, "L" for listening, "Q" for questioning, "C" for clarifying, and "S" for summarizing.

LESSON 27

COUNSELING SKILLS AND DIALOGUES

The skills that you have been working with are some of the most important skills in counseling. As you meet and talk with people in your daily activities, practice observing, listening, questioning, clarifying and summarizing.

At the same time, counselors avoid a number of things —
criticizing, arguing, and condemning. Also remember that
information learned in counseling is not public information, it is
knowledge should be kept confidential.

Questions:

1. During the coming week, try to use all five of the counseling
skills. Give an example from your daily activities of how you
have used each of the counseling skills.

2. Write a dialogue, a conversation between a counselor and
someone who is seeking help with a problem. Here are a few
guidelines to use:

> a. Focus on a problem or concern that someone is
>   sharing.
>
> b. Keep the dialogue simple.
>
> c. Bring the interaction, the dialogue, to some
>   conclusion. For instance, the counselor ended
>   with a summary and plans to visit Rose's place on
>   Saturday.

3. After you have written the dialogue, identify the parts that
show the counselor:

> O)   Observing
> L)   Listening
> Q)   Questioning
> C)   Clarifying
> E)   Summarizing

LESSON 28

PUBLIC VERSUS PRIVATE

When we greet people, no matter where we are, we need to be ready for any response. It could be a routine, familiar response:

Moruti (pastor): How are you?

Tabitha: I am fine. How are you?

Or the response could be one that is not so routine:

Moruti: How are you?

Tabitha: I am sick. I am sick of thinking about my friend and her family. Yesterday I was with her. She also must take care of her brother's children. His wife has died, and her brother has six children. There is no grandmother or auntie to help. Since I last saw you, Moruti (pastor),...

Yes, it is useful to be prepared for an answer different from a routine response. Sometimes those who are good listeners, counselors, find themselves in situations where someone like Tabitha is pouring out her heart. While it is helpful to listen, this may not be the time or place to hear all of Tabitha's worries. You might be expected somewhere else or Mrs. Brown, Rre Matumo's colleague, might be standing too close.

Moruti: Mma, we cannot talk about all of this right now in this shop. Could we meet at the church to visit? What time would suit you?

Tabitha: I can come at half past two.

Now that Tabitha can come this afternoon, the moruti can have the time to listen and to respond to her. A counseling session can be started by someone like Tabitha. It might be a good time for the counselor or it may not. The counselor needs to be alert and prepared to continue the discussion when it is convenient for both persons.

Questions:

1.   When will the moruti and Tabitha continue their talk?

2.   Why should Tabitha be encouraged to talk about her concerns at another time and in another place?

3.   What are other logical reasons for changing the time and place of a counseling session?

LESSON 29

THE PARTS OF A COUNSELING SESSION: 1

No doubt, the ability to listen is worthwhile. But many experts agree that there needs to be a structure for each counseling session, each time someone comes sharing a concern or problem. If there is no structure then somebody like Tabitha could do nothing but talk. There are people who describe one problem after another with little input from others and with little thought about solving problems.

Those who have done counseling for many years have found it helpful to divide the counseling session into parts. Doing this can provide structure and direction for both the counselor and the person with problems.

Counseling Session Parts:

A. Greetings
B. Purpose
C. Main Body
D. Close

E. Follow-up

Now let's look more closely at each part:

<u>Greetings</u>

When people meet each other they normally start talking with a greeting:

Moruti: How are you, Rra (Mr.)?

George: I am fine. How are you Rra?

This is an accepted way to start communications.

<u>Purpose Statement</u>

Each person has a reason for coming to see a counselor:

Rose: I am worried about my husband.

For some people it is easy to tell a counselor about their problems and worries. Still others, like Ketsile, may not be at ease. It is important to be patient and not push.

<u>Main Body</u>

Rose in Dialogue 1 tells Mma Tau why she is worried about her husband, Neo. She also explains how the children react to him and what he does to her.

This is an opportunity to ask questions and clarify what is being said. Looking at the dialogue with Rose, the counselor took advantage of this opportunity.

Questions:

1.   Why is structure important for a counseling session?

2.   In Lesson 27, you wrote a dialogue. Reread your dialogue and identify its parts:

G)   Greetings
P)   Purpose Statement
MB)   Main Body

LESSON 30

THE PARTS OF A COUNSELING SESSION: 2

A counseling session normally comes to a close or ending.

<u>Close</u>

The counselor ended Dialogue 1 with Rose by a) stating how she had helped her better understand her situation and b) telling her that she would come on Saturday. Mma Tau uses this time to review what has been learned and to say what happens next, two useful ways to end a conversation or counseling session. A prayer might also be added, seeking strength and insight.

<u>Follow-up</u>

After Rose left, Mma Tau wrote her name on a calendar by Saturday's date and the time she is to come to Rose's house, 3 p.m. This serves to remind the counselor of her promise to see Rose and Neo, something a busy counselor might need. Counselors who meet with many people might also need to keep notes of what has been talked about with each person. Such a notebook ought to be kept in a safe place so that others cannot read it. They can be useful but they must be carefully stored.

Questions:

1. Name two purposes for having a "close" in a counseling session.

2. Write a follow-up for the counseling session with Rose in Dialogue 1.

3. What does follow-up actually mean? What tasks need to be done by a counselor in a follow-up?

LESSON 31

DIALOGUE 2: AN EXAMPLE OF COUNSELING

Tabitha has come to the church.

Moruti: Good afternoon, Tabitha.

Tabitha: Good afternoon, moruti.

Moruti: You were talking about your friend this morning?

Tabitha: Yes, moruti. Yesterday, I was with her. She has three children, and she is also taking care of her brother's children. His wife has died, leaving six of them. Oh, moruti, there is no grandmother or auntie. Most of the family lives outside the country.

Moruti: Do you try to help?

Tabitha: Sometimes, but my own children and job make it difficult.

Moruti: It is good to talk about problems but it is even better to think about ways to solve them. Sometimes we are so busy talking about them that we forget that there are ways to solve them.

Tabitha: That can happen moruti.

Moruti: It is true that your friend has a major problem, and it is good that you are concerned. We need to think of ways of making her situation better. This week I would like for you to think about the ways that you and the church can be more helpful. Also, I want you to think about the things that your friend must do herself — that we cannot do for her.

Tabitha: I will, moruti. When shall we talk again?

Moruti: I will be here Wednesday in the morning.

Tabitha: Yes, moruti. I will see you on Wednesday.

The moruti closed the door after Tabitha left. He took out a small notebook and wrote, "see Tabitha on Wednesday." Then, "ask her about her assignment."

Questions:

1. Dialogue 2 may not have all of the parts of a typical counseling session. Which of the parts are present and which of the parts might be missing?

2. Using a G) for greeting, P) for purpose statement, MB) for main body, C) for close and F) for follow-up, show where these parts are at in Dialogue 2.

3. How does the follow-up in this Dialogue differ from the follow-up in Lesson 30?

LESSON 32

ASSIGNMENTS IN COUNSELING

At the end of Dialogue 2, the moruti gave Tabitha an assignment:

Moruti: This week I would like for you to think about the ways you and the church can be helpful to your friend. Also, I want you to think about the things that she must do herself — that we cannot do for her.

An assignment is a task for Tabitha, something that she must do outside of the counseling session. Tabitha has a habit of just talking about her problems — but not doing anything about solving them. The moruti knows this from past meetings with her.

In counseling, it is important for the person sharing her problems to take action, to do something constructive about solving them. It also gives the person with problems a chance to participate in the counseling process. At times, the most important part of the process takes place outside of the counseling session. After all, most problems are not solved in the counseling session. They are solved by troubled individuals who a) think or reflect about the problem, b) think about the source of the problem and c) take some action to improve the situation.

Questions:

1. What was Tabitha's assignment?

2. Why did the moruti give Tabitha an assignment?

3. Reread Dialogue 1. Write an assignment for Rose— one that would have been appropriate.

LESSON 33

A USEFUL REMINDER FOR COUNSELING SESSIONS

The parts of the counseling session can serve as a guide to you, the counselor. For new counselors, it is useful to write down the parts of a counseling session on a piece of paper and to keep them visible during each counseling session. It is a way to help you guide the discussion.

Now that you have seen examples of how a counseling session can be divided into parts, it is time for you to write another dialogue. Be sure to include an assignment.

Questions:

1. Think of a problem and write a dialogue of a counseling session. Identify each of the following parts:

G)   Greetings
P)   Purpose Statement
MB)   Main Body
C)   Close
F)   Follow-up

2. What is the assignment?

LESSON 34

DIRECTIVE COUNSELING

We have learned about five skills in counseling. We have also learned how the parts of a counseling session can give structure and guide discussion. Now lets look at two basic counseling approaches: directive and non-directive. In directive counseling, the counselor assumes that he or she knows what the problem is and how to solve it. Dialogue 3 is an example of directive counseling.

Dialogue 3

Lekoto: How are you?

Moruti: I am fine. How are you?

Lekoto: I am not so good today? I am looking for work. Do you have any work for me? I can wash your car. I can do all kinds of work. Please. I am hungry. I am looking for any kind of work.

Moruti: Come in. Where are you from?

Lekoto: I am from Serowe.

Moruti: Do you have a wife and children?

Lekoto: Yes, moruti. My family is in Serowe.

Moruti: Did I not see you near the shebeen by the taxi rank yesterday?

Lekoto: Yes. Beer is good for you.

Moruti: That is your real problem. Your waste your money on alcohol. It is really a sin. Ask God to forgive you of your sins. Perhaps if you didn't drink, God would help you find a job.

The moruti prayed. Lekoto left, his heart heavy with unhappiness and still with no job, and hungrier than ever. In directive counseling, the counselor is the authority. Thus, he or she gives advice and direction to those in need. That is, the counselor identifies the "real problem" and provides an answer.

Questions:

1. What is directive counseling?

2. Did the moruti in Dialogue 3 actually help Lekoto? Why or why not?

LESSON 35

NON-DIRECTIVE COUNSELING

In contrast to directive counseling, in non-directive counseling the counselor believes that the person who has come for help can identify the problems. That is, the person in need is the best source of information about what is happening. Answers to problems can also be found by the person in need. The job of the counselor is to help him find his own answers. The talk between Lekoto and the moruti could have been different.

Dialogue 4

Lekoto: How are you?

Moruti: I am fine.

Lekoto: I am not so good today. I am looking for work. Do you have any work for me? I can wash your car. I can do all kinds of work. Please, I am hungry. I am looking for any kind of work.

Moruti: Please come in and sit down. What kind of work have you been doing?

Lekoto: I was working at a construction site making wooden molds for pouring concrete (cement).

Moruti: Have you done any other kind of work?

Lekoto: Yes, I can lay bricks. I even have a certificate.

Moruti: Have you been to all of the building sites in town?

Lekoto: No, I just came from Francistown two days ago, and I might not have been to all of them. Are there any on this side of town?

Moruti: There are two just near us. Do you have your certificate with you?

Lekoto: No, I left it at a friend's house. I could go get it.

Moruti: That is a good idea.

Lekoto: Once I get the paper, I can go to sites on this side of town.

Moruti: Can you come back and let me know how it goes for you?

While this is not a complete counseling session, it does illustrate non-directive counseling. Instead of acting as the authority, the moruti helped Lekoto to think of his own solutions. The counselor did not have all the answers to Lekoto's needs.

Questions:

1. In which dialogue did the moruti give Lekoto more time to talk about his problems?

2. What do you think Lekoto would have done after Dialogue 4?

3. What is non-directive counseling?

LESSON 36

DIFFERENCES IN COUNSELING APPROACHES

Directive and non-directive counseling are different. In directive, the counselor assumes the role of authority. In non-directive the counselor lets the troubled person find their own solutions to their difficulties.

Since you have read Dialogues 3 and 4, you can see and read differences between both counseling approaches. They can also be seen in earlier case studies and dialogues. Now is your chance to prove that you understand the differences.

Questions:

1. Identify the counseling approach used in each of the following places:

      a.   CASE STUDY 1:

      b.   CASE STUDY 2:

      c.   CASE STUDY 3:

      d.   Dialogue 1:

      e.   Dialogue 2:

2. In earlier lessons you have written dialogues. Are yours more directive or more non-directive?

      a.   Reread your work for Lesson 27.

      b.   Reread your work for Lesson 33.

3.   Write a brief non-directive dialogue.

LESSON 37

**CASE STUDY 7: MOTIVES IN DIRECTING OTHERS'
LIVES**

Rre Leetile sells fruit at the train station. Business can be very
good in the early evening when the train leaves the city. His
wife, Mpho, does much of the selling and his sister's son, Dikole,
helps her.

Dikole came to live with Rre Leetile when there was no room in
the schools near his home. Now Dikole goes to school, and he
has a place to sleep and food to eat. In turn, Rre Leetile does not
pay Dikole for his work.

This situation has existed for three years and soon Dikole must
sit for his exam, the one which would let him continue to study
in secondary school. One afternoon Dikole came to Rre Leetile
and said, "I need to study for my Junior Certificate Exam. By
working every afternoon and evening there is no time to study.
And, when there are a few minutes, I am often too tired."

Rre Leetile thought to himself, "Dikole is a good worker. If he
isn't at the train station, I will have to help Mpho more. Besides,
this boy will never pass his exam. If Dikole fails his exam, he
will stay here and retake it next year. That way he will work
longer for me."

Then Re Leetile said, "Dikole, your mother said you would work
for me while you went to school. That was the agreement. I
expect you to keep it. Be at the station after school."

Questions:

1.   Why does Dikole live with Rre Leetile?

2.   What do you think of Rre Leetile's motives? Do you know anyone who would respond to Dikole in the same way?

3.   How would Dikole have felt after listening to Rre Leetile?

LESSON 38

MOTIVES IN DIRECTING LIVES: A DISCUSSION

In Rre Leetile's village many kilometers away people try to live together in peace. The elders often try to solve problems while meeting the needs of many people. Peace is to be between families. It should be seen in their behaviour.

Before coming to the city, Rre Leetile was said to be proud and selfish. Financial success has made him more so. Directive counseling, in the hands of a person like Rre Leetile, is a way to control others. Later he told Dikole, "Dikole, your real problem is that you are lazy."

Any form of counseling can be used or misused. Misuse can be seen in the motives of the counselor. An effective counselor listens and sees importance in the needs of others. As a consequence, a person like Rre Leetile would not be an effective counselor for Dikole since he serves his own interests not Dikole's.

This course stresses non-directive counseling. Directive counseling, while it has advantages at times, is also very easy to misuse. This is especially true where people live with rapid change. Many family problems were once solved in traditional ways using a more directive approach. Now problems can be solved many ways. Tradition, at times, can supply only part of the answers.

Questions:

1. Why do you think Rre Leetile told Dikole, "Your real problem is that you are lazy."

2. What is a primary reason for the misuse of different forms of counseling?

LESSON 39

DIRECTIVE COUNSELING AND COLONIALISM

Many people came to southern Africa. Some were from central Africa, some were from Europe. When the Europeans came, some of them sought to control everything. They took the best land, set up farms and opened mines. In almost every activity the Europeans did what they wanted to do with little or no regard for the rights of those who had lived there for generations. Asking Africans about African goals and objectives was not considered important. Many were much more concerned about using cheap African labor to achieve their own objectives, to expand their own wealth and power.

This changed an earlier pattern. In many African groups the chiefs and elders had listened to the problems of their people. The powerful once had responsibilities for the general well-being of all. Under the Europeans many of the common people were told to do things with little concern for what would happen to them.

"In general, taxation in the colonies was aimed at forcing the colonized people to work for the Europeans. The introduction of taxation also led to the impoverishment (making poor) of those who had few cattle. Those who did not find work had to sell cattle to pay the tax. Because the price of cattle was low, they sold many cattle in order to raise money for the tax. As time passed fewer and fewer people owned cattle. Many people became very poor."[1]

In addition, city life can give people like Rre Leetile greater freedom to do as they wish.

Questions:

1. How is the motivation of Rre Leetile similar to that of many European colonialists?

1. See pages 181 and 182 of Thomas Tlou and Alec Campbell's *History of Botswana*.

LESSON 40

LETTER 1: SHARING INFORMATION

Dear Brother,

Manaka, you have been away for three years and many things have happened. I want to share some secrets with you. I am worried and very afraid.

As you know I have three children with my wife, Moremi, and one with her sister, Jean. My wife doesn't know about me being the father of Jean's child.

Jean has left her husband to marry me, but my wife doesn't know anything about this. I no longer love my wife and I have asked Jean to marry me. Moremi is not the type of woman for me. She goes to parties when I am out of town. She probably even goes to shebeens without me.

I am being threatened by Jean's former husband. He says if he sees me with her he is going to "kill me." But I am so in love with her.

Manaka, I don't know what to do. Should I leave my wife and marry her sister or should I just go ahead and marry Jean? Should I try to stay away from Jean because of her old husband? Please tell me what you think.

Your worried brother, Kabo

Questions:

1. Kabo has a number of problems. Name them:

2. How should Manaka respond to his brother?

LESSON 41

REASONS FOR CONFIDENTIALITY

"Telling a secret to an untrustworthy person is like carrying maize in a bag with a hole." African saying.

Kabo did not want many people to know about his problems. And, at the same time, Manaka knew Kabo was in serious trouble, needing real help.

Many people with problems want and need to talk with someone who can listen to them. At the same time, it is important to many troubled individuals that the listener, the counselor, maintains confidentiality. That is, the counselor does not tell others about the problems. The church counselor keeps things secret and does not talk about what has been shared by people who come for help.

In an earlier lesson, you read about the qualities that a counselor should have. It is important that a church counselor be a good listener and be someone who can be trusted. Would we want to share our concerns with someone who would tell all our neighbors? Those looking for counseling need to know that what they say to the counselor will be held in confidence — will not be shared with others.

Questions:

1.   What is confidentiality? Write a definition of confidentiality. (Read Lesson 11 again.)

2.   Why is confidentiality so important to some people? Give at least two reasons why Kabo would not want his neighbors to know about his situation.

LESSON 42

CASE STUDY 8: MORE PROBLEMS FROM SHARING

Many things can happen when a person is untrustworthy and can not keep secrets. Manaka, the brother, was not sure what to tell Kabo. Both brothers were members of a church that does not approve of polygamy.

A few days after Kabo's letter arrived, Manaka saw their moruti on a street. The moruti was traveling to a regional church meeting. "Moruti, I need your advice. Please do not tell anyone about this but I am not sure what to do. I am afraid for what is happening to my brother, Kabo."

So Manaka told the moruti everything. The moruti was shocked. "Kabo had always seemed like a good Christian. Your brother is talking about marrying Jean. This is very wrong. Besides, he has committed adultery. No wonder Jean's former husband is mad. I am sure God is too."

The next Sunday the moruti spoke about Kabo in his sermon. "God knows all of your secrets. You need to ask his forgiveness."

Within a few hours of the sermon, Moremi and Jean had an awful fight. The entire village heard them.

Jean's former husband went away that very night. He is looking for the most powerful *moloi* (person who uses bad magic) in his district.

Questions:

1.   How do you think Kabo felt about the moruti? What do you think he did next?

2.   How unusual was the moruti's behaviour?

3.   Given what the moruti has done to Kabo, Jean and Moremi, it is likely that other people will bring their problems to him? Why or why not?

LESSON 43

CASE STUDY 9: DESTROYING CONFIDENTIALITY AND LIVES

Kabo was not in church to hear the moruti's sermon about him, Jean and Moremi. He heard within a few minutes after the service ended. Kabo had never been so upset in all of his life. "How did the moruti learn about us? Why did he tell everyone? Jean's husband will kill me for sure. He will drink too much and come looking for me."

Kabo disappeared from the village. He did not wait to see Moremi's anger, nor her fight with Jean.

A year has passed and Kabo has not returned to the village. Some people think he has left the country. Still others think he will never return. Perhaps the moloi did something. In any case, both Moremi and Jean have had a very difficult year, trying to feed their children.

Questions:

1. Both Manaka and Jean blame the moruti for what has happened. Do you agree with them? Why or why not?

2. Who else suffers? Jean, Kabo, Manaka and Moremi are not the only ones.

LESSON 44

LACK OF CONFIDENTIALITY LEADS TO NO COUNSELING

When someone comes to see a counselor, it's the responsibility of the counselor to discuss confidentiality. It is important for the counselor to tell the person that they will not share with others unless given permission. The very first time that someone comes to see a counselor is the time that the counselor needs to talk about confidentiality.

One of the common reasons for not sharing one's problems with a pastor is the inability of pastors to keep from talking to others. They are limiting their ability as shepherds while causing pain to others.

Confidentiality should be regarded as a basic part of counseling. It is a promise that a counselor makes to people with problems. To violate confidentiality is to betray the trust of people.

Questions:

1.   When should confidentiality be discussed in a counseling session?

2.   Why are problems often not shared with pastors?

3.   Who is promising to remain silent?

LESSON 45

CASE STUDY 10:   FEELINGS AT THE DEATH OF A PARENT

Jesse never thought much about his father dying. The older man, Ken Pulanka, was taller than most men and had large muscles from heavy construction work. Ken never seemed to be ill, year after year. Jesse almost believed that his father might outlive him.

Several months ago Ken woke up very early one morning at 3 a.m. His arm and shoulder were hurting. The pain was very great and very strange. Ken had not done any lifting or carrying in over week. He died shortly after getting to the clinic. The doctor said it was a heart attack, a massive one.

Jesse was surprised at Ken's sudden death and at his own feelings. The situation bothered Jesse very deeply. For this reason, Jesse went to talk to his moruti, Rev. Kgosietsile. Both men talked for over an hour. Jesse told the moruti about his concern. Rev. Kgosietsile listened thoughtfully, and at one point said that "the death of one's father can affect someone very deeply." Jesse went on doing most of the talking, and he gradually began telling the moruti about growing up.

Years ago Ken often worked in South Africa. He came home very seldom. When he did, it was awful. "My father beat me almost every day — most of the time without any reason. Ken had a violent temper, and he used it on his family. I cannot count the times he got drunk and beat my mother."

Rev. Kgosietsile commented. "Your father was a difficult person. Perhaps that explains some of your feelings at this time. Tell me more about him."

Since the moruti was a pleasant and calm person, Jesse kept talking. Finally, he said, "I am upset. I am surprised at my feelings. I always thought I would not be bothered with Ken gone. I actually hated him." Then moruti said, "Your feelings are understandable. Working in South Africa teaches people many things. Violence is one of them. Living there probably made his problem worse. I am glad you came to talk with me."

Questions:

1.   Why did Jesse dislike his father?

2.   How did Rev. Kgosietsile react when Jesse expressed his true feelings about his father?

LESSON 46

CASE STUDY 11: UNCONDITIONAL ACCEPTANCE

In Case Study 10, Rev. Kgosietsile is a good listener who accepts all of Jesse's feelings. The moruti never changed his attitude toward Jesse even when he said he hated his father. Rev. Kgosietsile was kind and understanding, never critical or harsh. Rev. Kgosietsile thought that for Jesse to get to the bottom of this situation he must be free to sort through his feelings.

Rev. Kgosietsile is practicing what is known in counseling as "unconditional acceptance." This implies that the counselor values the troubled individual regardless of their behaviour or feelings. Jesse feels comfortable with his moruti, and the moruti's attitude towards him never changes. Rev. Kgosietsile knows that God values even the worst sinner. The moruti also knows that Jesse is a child of God despite his relationship with Ken. Unconditional acceptance implies a willingness to value an individual even when they have done awful things — killed another person, robbed someone, or taken his cattle.

One of the purposes of counseling is to increase a person's understanding of problems. One way for Jesse to learn, and understand more about his relationship with his father, is to be able to express his feelings openly. Unconditional acceptance gives the troubled person a chance to talk about his concerns.

Questions:

1.   What is unconditional acceptance?

2.   Name two purposes of using unconditional acceptance.

3.   What scriptures support the use of unconditional acceptance?

LESSON 47

CASE STUDY: A FURTHER EXPLORATION OF FEELINGS

Jesse came and talked three more times with Rev. Kgosietsile. For a long time Jesse was puzzled about his feelings for his dead father. While he was upset, he was not sure why.

Jesse continued talking and the moruti continued to listen. At one point, the moruti mentioned ancestors, but this was not a big part of Jesse's worry. Jesse thought, "Ken, himself, never put much belief in that kind of thing. For some reason I am like Ken on this topic. Perhaps it comes from my training in science."

Later, Jesse began talking about Ken's stories. Ken liked to talk about some of his bosses in South Africa and the tricks played upon them. "Ken was a lot smarter than most of them. He made up poems to tell what he had done, and then he would tell them to his friends. Everyone would laugh and laugh."

As Jesse continued, he mentioned other things than Ken used to do. In spite of Jesse's general negative feelings he also had some positive ones as well. "I have a good mind like Ken." This discussion made Jesse feel better, and it led in an interesting direction. "Did you know that I even get mad — almost as mad as Ken? Yesterday I even found myself yelling at my son."

Questions:

1. Name three ways Jesse is like his father.

2. What puzzled Jesse after Ken's death?

3. What effect did talking with Rev. Kgosietsile have on Jesse?

LESSON 48

UNCONDITIONAL ACCEPTANCE AND DENIED FEELINGS

In Case Study 11, Jesse continues to explore his relationship with Ken and a number of thoughts he has about his father. Jesse started talking about some of Ken's better characteristics, including his sharp mind and sense of humor.

By the end of the case study, Jesse is beginning to explore feelings and behaviours that have been denied. Denied feelings are ones that a person does not recognize or does not see in a clear way. Jesse has not truly seen part of his own behaviour. He is bothered in a deep way about himself. "Unconditional acceptance" is giving Jesse the chance to think about things — things which threaten how he feels about himself.

Questions:

1.   One of the major sources of problems for people is denial. What is it?

2.   Why does denial happen?

LESSON 49

CASE STUDY 12: JESSE'S REAL PROBLEMS

By the end of his talks with Rev. Kgosietsile, Jesse realized more clearly one of his own problems. "I have a bad temper. It is almost as bad as Ken's." Ken's death reminded Jesse of one his own deepest fears. "I could end up like Ken. I do not want to be hated by my own son."

Now that Jesse recognized one of his most basic problems, he began thinking of ways to work on his temper. At least he wasn't combining it with lots of beer. Jesse also began to realize something else. When growing up his mother always told Jesse, "You are different from Ken. You do not have a temper." His mother hoped that by saying these things that Jesse would grow up different from his father.

Today Jesse continues watching for his own temper and tries to put limits on it. "I can make things better by working on my problems — but I must see it as it is."

Jesse no longer feels so negative about Ken. "I was more like him than I realized. I have forgiven him, and I have asked to be forgiven."

Questions:

1.   What is Jesse's deepest fear? Name the reason Jesse was so bothered by his own father's death.

2.   What had Jesse's mother told him? Why?

LESSON 50

SOURCES OF DENIAL: FINDING WHOLENESS

In the process of counseling, Jesse has grown. A better understanding of himself is leading to change. He understands himself better and is using this knowledge to change his own behaviour. Jesse's children recognize the difference.

Each person has the ability to grow, develop and expand oneself. Rev. Kgosietsile has provided a fine environment for this to happen. From counseling, Jesse also realizes that his own feelings were part of the problem. This recognition helps Jesse to both forgive his father and to seek forgiveness. Rev. Kgosietsile feels certain that God has forgiven Jesse. Even reconciliation is possible — to be at peace within and with one's father.

A common source of denial comes from the ideas and information of other people. Jesse's mother sent messages to her son that he believed. "You are different from Ken." While Jesse was different, he still shared a bad temper. Taking ideas and information from other people can lead to problems. Jesse's mother had actually made the situation worse. The borrowing of such information is known as introjection--a common source of misleading ideas about oneself.

Questions:

1. What is introjection?

2. What made forgiveness possible for Jesse?

LESSON 51

CLIENT-CENTERED COUNSELING

In Case Studies 10, 11, and 12, Rev. Kgosietsile is using a type of non-directive counseling known as client-centered or person-centered counseling. In all of his talks with Jesse, Rev. Kgosietsile let him do most of the talking. Jesse is the person who determined what was going to be discussed. At several points the moruti asked Jesse to tell him more about his feelings. In addition, the minister also agreed with Jesse's basic thought that Ken "was a difficult person."

The task of the counselor is to encourage discussion, to communicate that the person's feelings are understandable, and to ask questions. At the same time, the counselor avoids any criticism of Jesse, never condemning him.

Ultimately the problem and what to do about it comes from the person who is experiencing the difficulties. Rev. Kgosietsile does not define the situation or tell Jesse how to solve his problems. In the process Jesse becomes free and better understands his relationship with Ken. Jesse is growing and becoming stronger. Rev. Kgosietsile acts as a helper in the counseling session — not an expert with all of the answers.

Questions:

1.   Client-centered or person-centered counseling has appeared in earlier case studies and dialogues. Reread Dialogue 4, Lesson 35. How many questions did the moruti ask? What were they?

2.   Who was the source of the answer to Lekoto's problem in Dialogue 4?

3.   In Case Study 2, Lesson 7, Rre Matumo's behaviour is similar to non-directive counseling. How? Name two similarities.

LESSON 52

CARL ROGERS

Client-centered counseling began from the work of an American psychologist, Carl Rogers. Carl Rogers developed his ideas over thirty years of practice in counseling at clinics and universities. Many of the basic ideas in Lesson 45-50 come from his works: unconditional acceptance, denial, and introjection.

While many ideas about counseling began with medical doctors and from counseling the mentally ill, Rogers' own background is very different. He was raised in a Christian family and later even studied at a seminary. It is not surprising that relationships exist between Rogers' thinking and Christianity. He believes that people can change, becoming more whole. A warm and positive relationship between a counselor and another person can help make this happen. Rogers is optimistic about people and their ability to grow and change.

Questions:

1. How is Carl Rogers different from other experts on counseling?

2. How was unconditional acceptance a part of Jesus' ministry?

LESSON 53

THINGS TO BE SAID AND THINGS NOT TO BE SAID

The encouragement of growth is based upon communication in counseling. The use of unconditional acceptance in client-centered counseling implies that some things should be said. Questions can be asked. Words of encouragement and understanding are spoken. "Your problems are very real." "It is understandable why you feel that way." At the same time, unconditional acceptance makes the use of some words undesirable. There is no room for criticism, condemnation or rejection. Words such as "ought," "never," "must," are seldom if ever used.

Since the person with the problems finds their own answers in counseling, the counselor does not give orders or lots of directions. Expressions such as "you should," "you cannot," "start," or "stop" have little place in client-centered counseling.

Questions:

1. Write four things that you might say as a counselor during client-centered counseling.

2. Write four things that are not likely to be said by a counselor during client-centered counseling.

LESSON 54

COMMUNICATION AND UNCONDITIONAL ACCEPTANCE

Communications is important. While messages can be sent through speaking, they are also communicated through facial expressions and gestures, examples of non-verbal communication. Anger can be expressed in a person's eyes, in the shaking of her fist, or in the pointing of a finger. Nervousness might be seen in how a person smokes his cigarette, wrings his hands, or perspires. Communication in body language can also show positive feelings. Joy can be seen in a person's smile or the warmth of their handshake.

It is important that the counselor recognize both the verbal and non-verbal messages they are sending to the person who has problems. Unconditional acceptance implies that both types of communications are sending the same kind of message. It is not desirable to mix them. Positive words should be matched with positive expressions; both should agree.

Being alert to one's own feelings is important during counseling sessions. If the person's problems are too difficult for the counselor, then the counselor should consider sending that person to somebody else.

Questions:

1. Can you describe a situation where non-verbal communication does not match verbal communication?

2. Why should such situations be avoided in client-centered counseling?

LESSON 55

PERSON-CENTERED COUNSELING AND AGAPE

It has been said that person-centered counseling is an expression of agape — a love that liberates and can make people whole. The counselor, by not narrowly controlling the counseling session, opens discussion in such a way that the holy spirit enters. At the beginning of the talks with Jesse, Rev. Kgosietsile did not know what was at the center of Jesse's problems with Ken. And Jesse himself was not truly aware of the situation. Yet their discussions led to understanding, making life better for Jesse and his family.

Read the lesson about agape. See Lesson 12.

Questions:

1.   How did the moruti use agape in counseling with Jesse?

2.   How have you communicated agape to other people?

LESSON 59

A BEGINNING

This course is a beginning, a starting point for pastors and church workers learning about counseling needs. Rather than providing easy answers to problems that arise among individuals and families, this course challenges pastors to let answers emerge from their own congregations.

Throughout Africa there has been a concern for harmony among families, within communities and between people and God. Christianity has strength and vitality, reflected in the number of people who say that they are Christians and by church attendance.

To expect meaningful and appropriate answers to come from Africans, sisters and brothers in Christ, is to believe in the holy spirit working in people's lives. "Seek and Ye shall find."

The next lessons are intended to identify topics which African pastors and church workers are likely to face. Each example suggests the need for counseling.

1. Suicide

2. AIDS
3. Refugees
4. Families

Questions:

1. Give three reasons why the answers to counseling needs can emerge from African pastors and church workers.

2. What topics could you add to the four listed above? (Situations where counseling might be helpful?)

LESSON 60

CASE STUDY 14: SUICIDE

You have been asked to see the assistant superintendent of police, Rre Mujuru. He looks unhappy and uncertain. He begins to explain a dreadful concern, saying, "This last month there were four suicides in this district and two in this town. In this month last year there was only one. What is happening?"

Yesterday, deacon, I was called to a location six kilometers north of town. There was a 13 year old girl. She may have been pregnant. The girl has been wearing a fancy new dress and has been seen with a married man. Now she is dead. There are more young people killing themselves than have been dying in automobile accidents. Deacon, what is happening to our country? What should be done? I am tired of looking at bodies — some are hardly more than children. Yet it is not just the youth. One man was at least fifty. What should be done?"

Questions:

1. Why, based upon your knowledge, do people commit suicide?

2.   What things could church organizations do to reduce suicide in your community?

3.   How could you be helpful to Rre Mujuru?

LESSON 61

CASE STUDY 15: AIDS

When Sister Deborah Mokewa came to the house she knew that Mary had been sick. Even so, she was surprised at Mary's appearance. The once very attractive woman had lost at least 10 kilos, making her large sad eyes look even larger. Dark spots could be seen on her cheeks.

Then Mary began to speak in a very soft voice, "I am very weak. I want to go home to my village and to my parents. Yet I am both afraid and ashamed. A doctor believes I have AIDS. If it is true, I don't want to die away from home. But if I go home, my family would learn that I have been a prostitute. In the past there was no work, and I did not do it for very long. Sister what should I do? There are days when I feel too weak to ride the bus. What if I died on the bus? My heart is broken. Will my shame break my parents' heart? What should I do?"

Questions:

1.   Write a response to Mary's question.

2.   What choice or choices does Mary have?

3.   What can be done to help people with AIDS and their families in addition to prayer?

LESSON 62

CASE STUDY 16: THE REFUGEE SETTLEMENT

While Deacon Masuku had heard about the refugee settlement, it was from a member of his congregation that he began to learn more. A nurse who started working at the settlement began to tell him about the people who lived there. They came from all over Africa — Uganda, Liberia, Rwanda and other places. She told him stories of persecution, fear and violence — reasons given by many for leaving their homes. The stories moved Deacon Masuku's heart, and he decided to visit the refugees.

During the long, hot afternoon, Deacon Masuku listened to many people. One of whom told him, "Our village was surprised by armed bandits. They demanded food and beer. They took our chief, pointed a gun to his head and told everyone to bring food, to give it to them. When we brought them almost all we had, they were not satisfied. They began to shoot. People were being killed. We ran with the children into the bush. We walked for five days until we reached the border. We knew that near the border there were mines, bombs, planted in the ground. Even though we tried to move carefully, my wife stepped on one. It killed her instantly. Now my children have awful dreams and are afraid to go to sleep."

Another man shared with Deacon Masuku his reason for leaving home. He had been warned by a friend on the police force. "Your name," said the policeman, "is on a list. They plan to arrest and torture you."

Later, a deeply worried woman talked about her son. "He was taken from us by the police. We have not heard anything about him. Eight months have passed. Is he alive or dead?"

Questions:

1.   How did Deacon Masuku first hear about the lives of the refugees at the settlement?

2.   Why did the people Deacon Masuku talked to become refugees?

3.   Name four things which would make the lives of refugees difficult in a new place.

LESSON 63

BEGINNING TO HELP REFUGEES

It is not easy to leave one's home and move to a different place, even if one's life is threatened. One may have to learn another language, adapt to another climate, and learn how to live with the citizens of this "new" country. Added to this, refugees have to work with government workers to be classified as refugees — to receive what food, clothing and shelter that is available.

Going through these changes can lead to very real problems. Children, for example, may remember violence and destruction, leading them to behave "strangely." Some people become depressed. Others may have problems in family relationships as well as with people outside the family. Some may have fears about life in a new place and adjusting to it.

There are ways that Deacon Masuku is beginning to help refugees. First of all, he has been willing to listen to their stories, to learn of their worries and suffering. He is practicing agape. Through-out the scriptures Jesus encourages us to become involved in the healing of the hurt, the lost, and the lonely. (Luke 4:18-19)

Questions:

1.   Have you ever talked with a refugee? If so, what were his or her concerns and worries?

2.   Churches can help refugees in many ways. Name some ways.

3.   How can you help refugees?

LESSON 64

CASE STUDY 17: FAMILIES AND PROBLEMS

Rre Matumo's maid, Elizabeth, came to see him one afternoon when the teacher arrived at home. Elizabeth was worried. "Rre Matumo," she said, "The results have been announced from the Junior Certificate exam. My son, Trevor, has received a third class pass. It would be difficult to find a place for him in secondary school, and how could I afford the school fees? Trevor wants to look for work. He thinks he is too stupid to continue studying. Yet what is there to do with young people who are uneducated? The streets are full of them. I want him in school."

Then Rre Matumo said, "Many problems should be discussed within families. When can we meet with you, Trevor, and his older brother? If Trevor's father weren't working out of the country, we could include him as well. It could be helpful to talk about all of the possibilities for Trevor's future with all of the older family members together. Between sharing all of the choices, a practical solution might be found. The future of our young people is very important."

Rre Matumo is doing what some experts think is important. He is looking for answers to problems by bringing families together for discussions.

Questions:

1.   Can you think of a situation where a family has solved some problem by working together? What happened?

2.   This course has used 17 case studies. Name two case studies where counseling could have been done by bringing members of a family together. Explain.

LESSON 65

CONCLUSIONS

Church counseling is an expression of Agape for individuals and for families where there is some special concern. The concerns, as we have seen, range from alcoholism to the problems of refugees. They range from worries about school to worries about ancestors.

While prayer and preaching have an important role in the church, there are times when to be a good counselor is to be a good shepherd. May we be empowered in our ministries, serving the kingdom of Jesus Christ more completely.

LESSON 66

A DREAM FROM TALLAHASSEE, A DREAM FROM HARARE

When this counseling workbook was shared in Tallahassee, Florida, a church leader observed that the workbook could easily be adapted for use in United States. A comparable statement appears at the end of an April 2017 *Washington Post* article.[1] The statement came from a Zimbabwean psychiatrist, Dixon

Chibanda, after he finished describing a program he had designed and implemented in Africa.

In 2006, while starting to address the emotional needs of citizens in Harare, Zimbabwe, Chibanda soon realized that "25 percent of people suffered from depression and anxiety." In an attempt to help alleviate this suffering, Chibanda taught basic listening skills to 300 older women. As part of their training, the women learned to encourage people to share their problems. Chibanda believes that talking to a listener helps to reduce painful emotions generated by "thinking too much" about problems. Next, the women learned to encourage, when appropriate, the practice of "opening the mind," a response that can take place when people "identify their problems and feelings." Lastly, the older women learned to encourage "problem solving," a practice which offers a variety of ways to strengthen individuals who have discussed their problems with trained listeners.

After training, the older women are provided access to benches near health clinics. The benches, known as "friendship benches," offer places for people to come and share their problems. This service is important in a nation which has only "thirteen psychiatrists" for some 14 million residents. In the years since Chibanda's project began, the project has served "30,000 Zimbabweans."

Talking with a non-judgmental and discreet person opens the door for reflection upon problems and subsequent discovery of meaningful solutions. The Holy Spirit is freed to act in this process, transforming lives. The older women Chibanda has put near clinics in Zimbabwe provide valuable services to countless troubled people. Moreover, Dr. Chibanda believes that we could "plug" his friendship benches "into New York and get the same results."

If the congregation of every church in Africa included a few people trained in Church Counseling, these elders, deacons, and teachers could provide a listening service for their communities.

"Friendship benches" located in out-of-the-way spots or small rooms near churches in Africa would change lives for the better. Such a system here in America would transform lives as well. Hundreds of rural counties and small towns have neither a psychiatrist nor a psychologist! Listening skills offer congregations the empowering potential to mend lives in their communities. What a loving Christian gift!

1. "Facing a Suicide Crisis in his Country, This African Psychiatrist Enlisted Grandmothers to Step In," *Washington Post*, April 19, 2017.

Parting Wishes for You:

The authors are very aware that directive counseling is common in Africa: people want the person they go to offer suggestions on what they should do, as in the past when the elders would listen and give guidance/instruction on what ought to be done. The decision in this workbook to stress non-directive counseling is to widen the perspectives of readers while showing how directive counseling can be misused.

In the real world, non-directive counseling can be a phase in which the church counselor begins to understand the complicated nature of some problems. Once the counselor has reached an understanding of some depth, directive suggestions can be more effective. Of course, some programs such as Divorce Care and Alcoholics Anonymous have their own existing structures.

The authors hope that you will create new case studies in which church counselors shift from non-directive to directive counseling. Please have the church counselors address problems not mentioned in this workbook or handled superficially. Use your ideas to improve this work in multiple dimensions. *An Introduction to Church Counseling: From Africa, For Africa* is only a beginning! Please remake it into something far better!

9 781981 853847